D0432250

Lion Children's Favourites

30

Bible Stories and Prayers

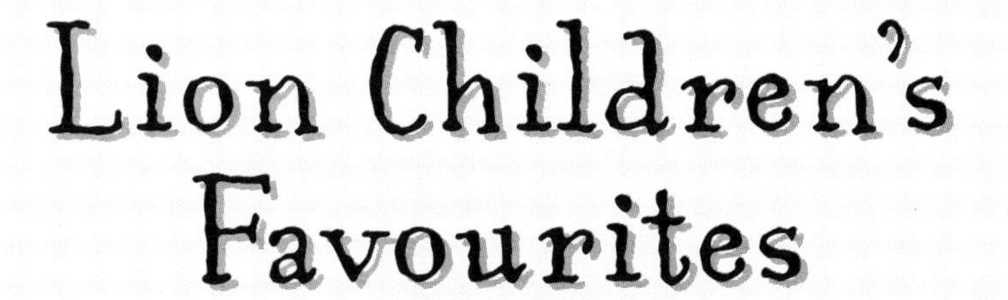

30

Bible Stories

and Prayers

Contents

In the Beginning

The creation story retold by Steve Turner
illustrated by Jill Newton

God said WORLD
and the world spun round
God said LIGHT
and the light beamed down

God said NIGHT
and the sky went black
God said LAND
and the sea rolled back

God said LEAF
and the shoot pushed through
God said FIN
and the first fish grew

God said BEAK
and the bright birds soared
God said FUR
and the jungle roared

God said SKIN
and the man breathed air
God said BONE
and the girl stood there

God said GOOD
and the world was great
God said REST
and they all slept late

Thank You for Our World

Prayers by Alexander Carter and Naomi Smith
illustrated by Rhian Nest James

Father,
Thank you for the sun
which helps things grow.
Please help us always
to grow in love with you.
Amen.

Thank you, Lord,
for our world –
for the sun and moon.
Thank you, Lord,
for the seas and trees.
Thank you for the animals,
like birds and bees.
Mostly, Lord, thank you for us,
that we are alive and that we
have such a beautiful world.
Amen.

My Very First Noah's Ark Story

A retelling of the Bible story illustrated by Alex Ayliffe

Old Man Noah listens;

he hears the voice of God.

'My world has all gone bad;

I'm going to wash it in a flood.

So build an ark, long, wide and

high, your family and you...

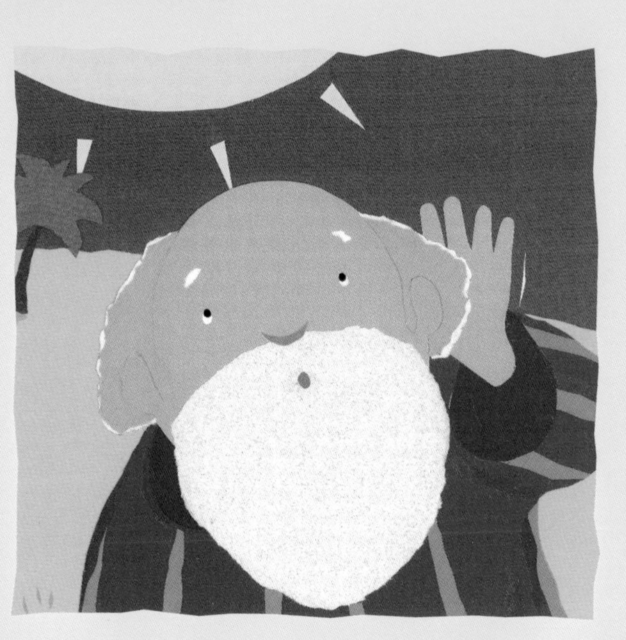

'And on it take your animals,

by two, by two, by two.

Fetch all the creatures of the wild –

the rabbit, deer and shrew...

The tiger and the elephant,

the snake and kangaroo.

Then every kind of bird must come,

to fill the ark with song.'

When Noah has them safe on board,

it rains both hard and long.

For days the big ark floats away,

then BUMP – it hits a peak.

A dove flies out, and then comes back,

a green leaf in its beak.

The waters trickle to the sea;

at last the land is dry.

God says, 'The flood is over.

See – my rainbow in the sky.'

A Prayer of Thanksgiving

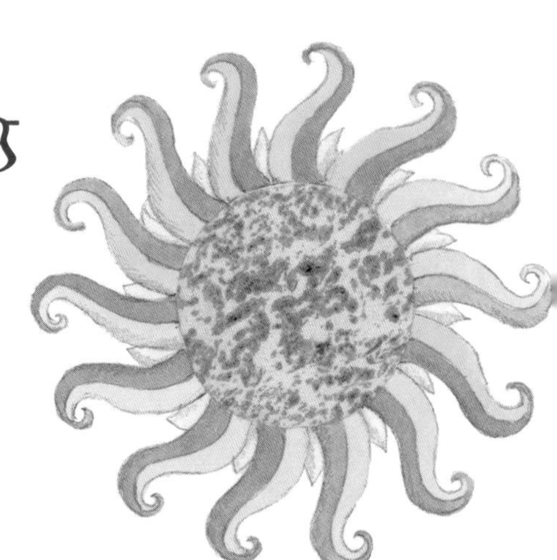

by Joyce Denham

illustrated by Helen Cann

I thank the God of Heaven
For rains that soak the Earth.

I thank the Creator of Earth
For food to nourish the World.

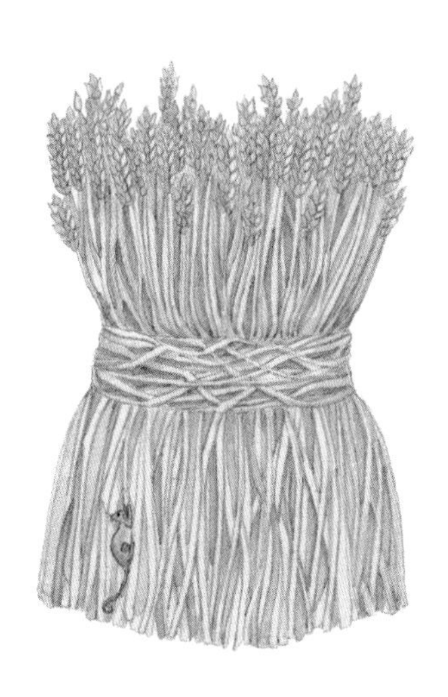

I thank the Saviour of the World
For fathers and mothers and children.

I thank the Friend of Children
For all the wonders of Life.

I thank the Spirit of Life
For His abiding Love;
For His abiding Love.

Mabel and the Tower of Babel

The Bible story retold
and illustrated by John Ryan

There was once a king and a queen who ruled over the whole world. They thought they were quite the most important people that had ever been.

But, actually, it wasn't *too* difficult to rule the whole world because at that time everybody spoke the same language.

The king and the queen used to pat one another on the back and tell each other how important they were. They told everybody else, too, and, because it is often the safest thing to do with kings and queens, everybody agreed with them.

The only person who didn't agree with them was their small daughter, Mabel.

Mabel was almost always right.

She said, 'Actually, Mama and Papa, you *can't* be the most important people because the most important of all has to be God.'

'Rubbish!' said the queen. '*Who* is this God of yours?'

'God made the world and everyone in it,' answered Mabel.

'Stuff and nonsense!' spluttered the king. 'You may think you're right, Mabel, but you're wrong this time. *Where* is this God of yours?'

'Everywhere,' answered Mabel. 'And up there especially, I think,' she added, pointing to the clear blue sky.

'We'll soon see about that,' said the king.

'We will indeed!' said the queen. 'Only, how?'

'We'll build a tower, the biggest and tallest tower ever made,' replied the king. 'A tower so high that it will reach all the way to God – if there is such a person. *Then* we'll see who is the most important!'

'It won't work,' said Mabel, who was almost always right.

So the king sent for his chief builders and told them about the tower. It was to be the biggest and tallest building ever made. Together they worked out how to build it.

Next day, they started work. Thousands of trees were chopped down…

Huge quantities of bricks were baked. Everything was brought to the spot chosen by the king.

Just about everybody who was fit to work was made to help.

Slowly the enormous tower began to rise from the ground.

Every day it got bigger and taller… and bigger and taller and taller…

And every day Mabel came out and looked at it and said, 'It won't work, you know!'

At last the great tower was finished.

'Now,' said the king to the queen. 'Let us climb to the top with all the people.

'When we get there, first we will declare the tower open. Then we'll see if there's any sign of this God that Mabel is always talking about!'

'I think you're going to be sorry about this,' said Mabel.

So the king and the queen climbed all the way to the top of the enormous tower. It was a hot day and they were both red in the face when they got there.

All their subjects went up too. Everybody wanted to see their king open the tower and talk to God.

Just then God looked down from heaven and noticed the tower far below.

'Whatever is that extraordinary little pimple down there?' he asked one of the angels around him. 'It looks like an anthill.'

'It's a sort of tower, Lord,' said an archangel. 'The King of the Earth thinks that if he builds high enough, he will be as good as you.

'Shall we knock the tower down, Lord?' asked the archangel. 'I have a very handy-sized thunderbolt here.'

'No, no,' said God. 'That would never do. Somebody might get hurt and I'm really very fond of the people on Earth. I have a better idea. I'll make them all speak different languages. Then see what will happen!'

Far down below, at the very tiptop of the tower, the king was beginning his speech.

'Ladies and gentlemen,' he announced. 'This is a most important – perhaps the most important…'

But, even as he was speaking, the strangest thing happened…

Hardly anybody could understand a word the king said. Suddenly they were all thinking and speaking different languages of their own.

'Can't hear!' called some.

'Speak up!' cried others.

But most of them shouted, 'He's talking poppycock!' – which is not at all the way to address a king.

Moreover, most of the people couldn't understand what their fellows were saying either. There was a great deal of shouting and arguing and waving of hands.

Then everybody started to leave the tower, splitting into groups who found they *could* understand one another.

The king and the queen were left on the top of the tower. They watched their people trailing away into the distance in long straggling lines.

They were all going away to start countries of their own where they could all use the same words and have rulers whom they could understand.

'You see what I mean?' said God to the archangel. 'Otherwise the people on Earth will think they can get away with *anything*.'

The king and queen made their way down to join the few people who stayed loyal to them.

'It looks to me,' said the king, 'as though we have a rather small kingdom now. I'm afraid that's the end of being the most important people in the world.'

'Told you so!' said Mabel. 'You can't beat God!'

And that was the end of the story – except that they called the tower 'Babel', which means a lot of loud, meaningless words. It also happens to rhyme with Mabel.

After a while it fell down, because there weren't enough people around to keep it up.

And Mabel, who was almost always right, rather wished she hadn't been this time.

It was such hard work trying to learn all the new different languages!

Joseph

The Bible story retold by Felicity Henderson
illustrated by Toni Goffe

Long ago, in the land of Canaan, there lived a man called Jacob.

He had twelve sons. They all worked hard, looking after their father's sheep.

Benjamin was the youngest son. But of all his sons, Jacob loved Joseph best.

One day Jacob gave Joseph a beautiful coat. This made the other brothers jealous.

'We work harder than he does,' they said. 'Why should Joseph get all the best things? Why does our father love him more than us?'

One night Joseph dreamed that his family were sheaves of wheat in a field. His sheaf stood up straight while all the others bowed down to it.

His brothers were annoyed when he told them about the dream.

Later Joseph made his brothers even more angry.

'I had a dream last night,' he said. 'I dreamed that the sun and the moon and eleven stars bowed down to me.'

'Be quiet!' replied his brothers. 'We are not going to bow down to *you*.'

Joseph's brothers got tired of his dreams. And even his father told him to keep quiet.

'That's enough, lad,' he said sharply. But secretly Jacob wondered about his son. Although Joseph was boastful and proud, could God have a special job for him, when he was grown-up?

One day Jacob sent Joseph to find his brothers. They were far from home, looking after the sheep.

It was a long journey.

The brothers saw Joseph coming, wearing his special coat. Then they remembered that their father loved him most.

'Here comes the dreamer!' said one of them.

'The big-head!' said another.

Some of the brothers hated Joseph so much that they made a plan to get rid of him.

'I'm fed up with the way Father listens to him,' said one. 'Him and his fancy coat!'

At last Joseph arrived at his brothers' camp. He had brought them some lovely food from home and he wanted to tell them all the news.

But, before he could open his mouth, some of the brothers pulled off his special coat and threw him into a deep dry well.

They sat down to eat the food and took no notice of his cries for help.

Just then the brothers saw some camels in the distance.

'Those traders are on their way to Egypt,' said one. 'Let's sell Joseph to them as a slave. They will take him far away and we can make some money.'

So the brothers sold Joseph to the traders. They were going to the far-off country of Egypt.

It was a long journey and Joseph wondered what would happen to him there.

Meanwhile the brothers were up to more mischief. They had kept Joseph's coat and put some blood on it. Then they took it home and told their father a wild animal had killed him.

Jacob was very upset. 'My poor boy!' he cried.

In Egypt Joseph became a slave to a very important man. Life was very different from when he had lived with his father and brothers. He wondered if he would ever see his family again.

Sometimes Joseph thought about all the things that had happened. Perhaps he had been too boastful about his dreams. He was sorry he had been so proud.

'I'm all alone,' he said sadly. But then he remembered that God was with him and he felt less lonely.

Joseph decided that now he would work hard to please both God and his master in Egypt. If he met his family again, he wanted them to be proud of him.

when Moses was a little boy, he floated down the river Nile.
then pharaoh's daughter found him there playing with his teddy bear.

Moses Hears God's Call

The Bible story retold by Pat Alexander
illustrated by Carolyn Cox

In the time of Joseph, Jacob's family moved to Egypt to escape a famine. Time passed, and Jacob's descendants – the Israelites – grew into a strong and powerful nation. The Egyptians began to be afraid of them. A new king came to the throne and he decided to act before it was too late.

He made the Israelites his slaves. Cruel slave-drivers forced them to make bricks to build new cities for the king. They were kept hard at work from dawn to dark – but still their numbers grew.

So the king gave orders that every Israelite baby boy should be drowned in the River Nile.

About this time an Israelite woman called Jochebed had a baby. She already had two children, a boy called Aaron, and a girl called Miriam. When she saw that the new baby was a boy she was terribly afraid. She hid him in the house for three months; but babies won't stay quiet and still for long. What was she to do?

Then she had an idea. She made a basket out of reeds and covered it with tar, to make it watertight. She put the baby inside. Then she took the basket and placed it among the tall reeds at the river's edge. She told Miriam to keep watch.

Very soon, the king's daughter came down to the river to bathe, as Jochebed knew she would. And when she saw the basket she sent her servant to fetch it. They opened the lid, and there inside was the loveliest baby she had ever seen. And he was crying! The princess knew that this was an Israelite baby. But she had no children and she decided to bring him up as her own son. She would call him Moses.

The princess turned and there, right beside her, was Miriam, offering to fetch a nurse for the baby. And of course the nurse Miriam ran to find was the baby's own mother!

So Moses grew up in the king's palace, learning all that the Egyptians could teach him. But he never forgot that he was an Israelite. And it made him sad to see how cruel the Egyptian slave-drivers were to his people.

One day he saw an Egyptian lashing one of the Israelites with a whip. Moses sprang at the man and killed him. Now his own life was in danger, for the king would hear what he had done. So Moses left Egypt and fled to the safety of the desert.

He was there a long time, working as a shepherd in the land of Midian. In Egypt the troubles of the Israelites grew worse.

One day, as Moses was out minding his father-in-law's flocks, he saw a very strange sight. There was a bush which seemed to be on fire. But the fire did not burn it up.

Moses went to have a closer look.

'Stand back,' said a voice. 'And take off your shoes – you are on holy ground.'

Moses was very afraid. The voice came again:

'I am God – the God your fathers knew and worshipped. I have seen the cruel sufferings of my people the Israelites. You are to go to the king of Egypt and set my people free. Bring them here to me.'

'But what am I to say? What am I to do? They won't listen to me,' said Moses. 'Please send someone else!'

'No,' said God. 'I have chosen you. Take your brother Aaron with you to do the speaking, and I will give you the words – and power to work wonders. Am I not the living God?'

Moses and Aaron stood before Pharaoh, king of Egypt.

'We have a request to make,' they

said. 'The Lord God of Israel says, "Let my people go out into the desert for a festival." '

'I don't know your God,' answered the king. 'What is he to me? I will not let the Israelites go.'

The king was angry.

'From now on no one is to give the Israelites the straw they need to mix with the clay to make their bricks,' he said. 'Let them find their own. And they must make just as many bricks as before.'

This was terrible. In despair, Moses cried out to God for help.

'You will see what I shall do to the king of Egypt,' God said. 'I am God. I shall make Pharaoh let my people go. I shall set them free and you will lead them out of Egypt. Go to the king again. Tell him I shall bring terrible trouble on Egypt if he will not do as I ask. Then all Egypt will know that I really am God.'

Moses and Aaron stood before the king again.

'Show me a miracle, if you really come from God,' he said.

So Aaron threw down the strong stick he carried – and it became a snake. But the Egyptian magicians did the same, so the king sent Moses and Aaron away.

Then God took action, as he had warned. Terrible things began to happen. Every time, God sent a warning to the king beforehand. But the king did not believe him. He would not listen, and he would not change his mind.

First the water in the River Nile turned blood-red. It smelt dreadful, and all the fish died.

A week later the whole land was swarming with frogs.

Next came swarms of insects and flies, and then the cattle began to die.

After that everyone had painful

boils, even the magicians.

Moses and Aaron went and stood before the king yet again.

'God says, "You have seen my power. There is more trouble to come if you do not let the Israelites go. Tomorrow there will be hail!" '

No one had ever seen hail like it. It flattened the crops and killed the cattle out in the fields.

Next came swarms of locusts, which ate up every green thing. And after that, pitch-darkness for three days. But the king still tried to bargain with God. He would not let the people go.

Then the most terrible thing of all happened. In a single night the eldest son of every family in Egypt died – from the king's son and heir to the son of his lowest slave.

But the Israelites were safe. God had told them what to do.

Every Israelite family killed a lamb that night, and splashed some of the blood on the doorposts of the house. They roasted the lamb and ate it with herbs and flat loaves of bread, made quickly without yeast. And death 'passed over' their houses. (That is why for ever after, once a year, the people of Israel ate this special 'Passover' meal, and remembered how God had saved them.)

Next day the Egyptians could not wait to get rid of the Israelites. They even gave them gold and silver jewellery and fine clothes to take with them.

But still the king tried to stop them. As soon as they had gone he called out the army. The soldiers leapt into their swift, light chariots and raced after the Israelites.

By the time the Israelites reached the lakes and marshes near the border, the Egyptian army was close behind. There was water in front of them, and soldiers behind them. The people were terrified.

But Moses stretched out his arm, and God sent an east wind. All night it blew, clearing a pathway through the water for the Israelites to cross in safety.

But when the Egyptians tried to follow, the water rushed back and the king's whole army was drowned. So God saved his people and led them out of Egypt to freedom.

The

Ten Commandments

A retelling of the Bible sayings for children
illustrated by Claire Henley

From the beginning, the Bible says, the good and right way for people to live is to love the God who made them and to love one another. This good and right way to live is set out in the Ten Commandments. These were laws that God gave a group of people called the Israelites thousands of years ago as they travelled from Egypt, where they had been slaves, to a land where they could be free: free to live as God wants.

I am God. I have always taken care of my people.
You must love and obey me only.

God spoke all these words, saying, 'I am the Lord your God, who brought you out of the land of Egypt... You shall have no other gods before me.'

Don't let anything be more important than me.
You shall not make for yourself graven images... you shall not bow down to them or serve them...

You must respect me, and take care how you speak about me.
You shall not take the name of the Lord your God in vain.

Keep my day of rest, one special day each week.
Remember the sabbath day, to keep it holy.

Show respect to your mother and father.
Honour your father and your mother.

Do not kill.
You shall not kill.

Husbands and wives: keep your special love just for each other.
You shall not commit adultery.

Do not steal.
You shall not steal.

Do not tell lies.
You shall not bear false witness against your neighbour.

Do not be greedy for the things other people have.
You shall not covet anything that is your neighbour's.

The Knock-out Story of David and Goliath

The Bible story retold by Nicky Farthing
illustrated by Bernice Lum

All the animals were gloomy.
'Fierce soldiers have come to take our land, our home,' announced King Hippo.
'Will anyone dare to fight them?'

I wish I was back in the jungle.

Um, they're bigger than me!

Er, um, no way!

Uh-oh!

The animals looked towards the army.
Then came a great shout.
I am GOLIATH. Who will dare to fight me? If you can find a CHAMPION who can beat me, then my army will leave, and your home will be safe.
Isn't there ANYONE who dares to fight him?

Out went David.
'Take care, little monkey,'
said the King.

Goliath was very angry.
He began to run towards David.
David reached for a stone.
Big bully! The Maker of the Jungle will help me beat you.
SPLAT!
The fierce animals all ran away with their tails between their legs.
Hooray for David!
David was carried high through the crowds.
'The Maker of the Jungle did help him!' all the animals cheered.
What a monkey!
Yeah!
Whoopee!

A Happy Day

Five everyday prayers
illustrated by Maureen Bradley

For this new morning with its light,
Father, I thank you.
For rest and shelter of the night,
Father, I thank you;
For health and food,
for love and friends
for everything your goodness sends,
Father in heaven, I thank you.

Thank you for each happy day.
For fun, for friends, and work and play;
Thank you for your loving care,
Here at home and everywhere.

Dear Lord Jesus, we shall have
this day only once; before it is gone,
help us to do all the good we can,
so that today is not a wasted day.

In our work and play God leads us,
Every step we take.
In our sleep he will be near us,
Watching till we wake.

The moon shines bright,
The stars give light
Before break of day;
God bless you all
Both great and small
And send a joyful day.

A Fishy Story

The story of Jonah retold by Pat Alexander
illustrated by Leon Baxter

Jonah was running away. He was running away to sea.

'Go to Nineveh,'* God said to Jonah. 'The people there are doing wicked things. Tell them to stop being nasty at once, or there will be trouble.'

Jonah did not want to do as God told him – so he ran away from God.

The people of Nineveh were the fierce enemies of Jonah's people, the people of Israel. Jonah wanted God to punish them.

If he went to warn them, they might stop being nasty. Then God would be kind to them.

Jonah did not want that. That was why he was running away.

The ship sailed away with Jonah on board.

*The capital city of enemy Assyria.

He was so tired, he fell fast asleep. He was *so* tired he didn't hear the wind blow, stronger and stronger. He didn't feel the waves rock and toss and throw the ship about. He didn't hear the sailors' frightened cries.

He did not know there was a storm – a very scary storm.

'Wake up! Wake up!' said the captain, shaking Jonah hard. 'Say your prayers, before we all drown!'

But Jonah was running away from God. How could he ask God to help him?

'It's all my fault,' Jonah said to the sailors. 'You must throw me into the sea.'

No one wanted to do that, but in the end they did. And at once the sea was calm.

Down, down, down Jonah sank. Deep down, beneath the waves. But God did not let him drown. God sent a great big fish, and…

GULP! GULP! GULP!

… Jonah was safe inside. It was dark and slippy and slimy in there. But Jonah was alive!

'You saved my life,' Jonah said to God. 'Thank you. I'm sorry I ran away. Next time I'll do as you tell me – if I ever get out!'

Jonah was stuck inside the fish for three whole days. Then…

HIC! HIC! HICCUP!

… the fish spat Jonah out on a nice dry beach.

Jonah took a BIG breath of fresh air. He held his face up to the warm sun. He wriggled his toes in the soft sand – and then he set off.

'God is going to *punish* you,' Jonah told the people of Nineveh. 'He knows all about you – every nasty little thing!'

Then the people of Nineveh were sorry. They stopped being nasty – and God was kind to them.

Jonah sat in the hot sun and sulked. He was *very* cross.

'I just knew this would happen,' he grumbled to God. 'I wanted you to *punish* those people! They are our enemies – they *deserved* to be punished!'

But God said: 'Think of all those children, and the animals too. I love *everyone* – yes, even the people of Nineveh. Isn't that a good thing?'

My Boat and Me

A prayer illustrated by Liz Pichon

Dear God, look from your heaven
Upon my boat and me,
Protect me from the billows
Of the great and stormy sea.

Daniel and the Lions

The Bible story retold by Bob Hartman
illustrated by Susie Poole

God was very sad. Most of his people had stopped listening to him, and talking to him, and following his rules.

'If you do not change your ways,' he warned them, 'you will have to leave this special country I gave you long ago.'

But the people would not listen. So God let their enemies defeat them, and destroy their cities, and carry them hundreds of miles away to be slaves in another land.

There were, however, a few of God's people who did not forget him. One of them was Daniel.

He worked hard in the new land – so hard that he became one of the king's own helpers! But he never forgot about God, or failed to pray to him, morning, noon and night.

Some of the king's men were jealous of Daniel. They wanted his job for themselves. So they talked the king into making a new law, a law which said, 'No one, but no one, is allowed to pray to anyone but the king himself.'

'We've got Daniel, now!' his enemies laughed.

And so they had. For the very next morning, Daniel knelt by his window, bowed his head and prayed – not to the king, but to God.

'Thank you for taking care of us in this faraway land,' he prayed. 'Forgive us, and please take us back to our own land, soon.'

Daniel's enemies were watching. And before he could even open his eyes, they grabbed him and dragged him in front of the king.

The king was sad. Very sad. He liked Daniel. But he could not break his own law.

'Daniel must be punished,' he sighed. 'Throw him into the lion pit.'

But even as the king gave the order, he whispered a prayer that no one could hear. A prayer to Daniel's God that, somehow, Daniel might be saved.

The pit was dark. The pit was deep. The lions covered its floor like a shaggy growling carpet. They leaped to their feet in a second when Daniel landed among them. They licked their lips. They showed their teeth. Their eyes shone bright and fierce. They opened their mouths and moved towards their dinner. And then they stopped.

'Shoo! Scat! Go away!' shouted a voice right behind Daniel.

The lions' mouths snapped shut. Their tails drooped. And they whimpered away to the corners of the cave.

Slowly Daniel turned around, and looked up into the face of an enormous angel!

'Nothing to worry about, now,' the angel smiled. 'God sent me to watch over you. Why don't you get some sleep?'

The next morning, the king cheered when he discovered that Daniel was still alive and walked him back to the palace.

Meanwhile Daniel's enemies cried for help. And the lions enjoyed their breakfast!

The World is Such a Wonderful Place

Two prayers by Mary Batchelor
illustrated by Alison Jay

I look around and the sun's in the sky,
I look around and I think oh my!
The world is such a wonderful place.
And all because of the Good Lord's grace.

We have so much to thank you for,
Our heavenly Father dear:
For life and love and tender care,
Through all the happy year;
For homes and friends and daily food,
Each one a gift of love.
For every good and perfect gift
Is from our God above.

The First Christmas

The Bible story retold by Penny Frank
illustrated by John Haysom

Long ago, before the first Christmas, there was a beautiful young woman called Mary.

She lived in the little town of Nazareth.

One day, when Mary was busy in her home, the room was suddenly full of bright light.

There, in the light, stood an angel of God. Mary was really frightened.

'Don't be afraid, Mary,' said the angel. 'The message I have for you is a message of joy. You are going to have a baby son.'

'But I have no husband,' said Mary.

'He will be the Son of God himself,' said the angel. 'You must call him Jesus.'

'I will do whatever God wants,' said Mary, and the angel went away.

There was a young man in Nazareth, called Joseph. He loved Mary. He wanted Mary to marry him.

The angel visited Joseph, in a dream.

'I have come to tell you that Mary is going to have a baby. He is the Son of God,' said the angel.

'You must call the baby, Jesus. He has come to save the whole world.'

Then the angel went away.

Mary and Joseph made their plans to get married. They loved each other very much. They often talked about the angel's message and about the special baby.

'Will people believe that Jesus is the Son of God?' said Mary.

'Don't worry,' Joseph said. 'Some people will understand. God promised he would send a special person to rescue the world. Now we can be glad that he has kept his promise.'

So Joseph and Mary waited for Jesus to be born. There were a lot of things to get ready for the baby. It seemed a long time to have to wait.

One day they heard that the Emperor who ruled their country had made a new law.

'Everyone must travel back to his home town to have his name written on a register,' Joseph told Mary. 'We will have to go all the way to Bethlehem.'

'I would have liked to stay at home to have my baby, but the prophets did say that God's Son would be born in Bethlehem,' said Mary, as the donkeys carried them on their journey.

'I am so tired,' she said. 'And it is such a long way.'

When they came to the town, it was very busy. So many people had come to register in Bethlehem that there was no room left in the inn.

But the innkeeper said they could use the stable where he kept his animals.

Joseph helped Mary down from the donkey and took her into the stable. Mary made a bed for them on the straw with her warm cloak. She knew her baby would soon be born.

When the baby was born, they wrapped him up warmly and made a place for him to sleep in the manger, where the animals' hay was kept.

'His name is Jesus,' they said. 'He is God's own Son.'

The animals stood watching them. Their warm breath filled the tiny stable.

It was not quiet for very long.

The stable door creaked open and some shepherds came in.

'Where is the baby?' they asked Joseph gently. 'Can we see him?'

'Of course,' said Joseph. 'But how did you know a baby had been born?'

'We were out on the hills with our sheep,' said the shepherds. 'Suddenly there was a bright light and God's

angels came to us. They told us there was a baby here who would grow up to save us all. And we came at once to find him.'

The shepherds went back to their sheep. They told their story to everyone they met.

Mary and Joseph stayed in Bethlehem for a while.

One day there was a knock on the door. Some important visitors stood outside.

'We have come a long way to see the baby king,' the wise men said. 'Is he really in here?'

'Yes,' said Joseph. 'But how did you know a baby had been born?'

'We saw a bright star in the sky,' they said. 'Our books showed us it would lead us to the baby born to be a king in Israel. So we followed it.'

The visitors knelt down by the baby and presented their gifts of gold, frankincense and myrrh.

When the visitors had gone, Joseph and Mary looked at their baby. They had so much to think about.

They remembered the angels who had come to the shepherds, and the bright star which had led the wise men.

They looked again at the beautiful presents.

'At last God has sent his Son to Israel,' said Joseph.

'Yes,' said Mary, 'to Israel and to the whole world. Those wise men came from far away. Maybe they need him there too.'

Joseph and Mary thanked God for the baby Jesus. They knew that God had kept his promise to send his Son to save the whole world.

They did not understand yet what work God had for Jesus to do. But they knew that he would show the world what God is like.

Silent Night

The carol arranged by Philip and Victoria Tebbs
illustrated by Francesca Pelizzoli

Silent night, holy night,
All is calm, all is bright
Round yon virgin mother and child;
Holy infant so tender and mild,
Sleep in heavenly peace,
Sleep in heavenly peace.

Silent night, holy night,
Shepherds quake at the sight;
Glories stream from heaven afar,
Heavenly hosts sing alleluia;
Christ, the Saviour, is born,
Christ, the Saviour, is born.

Silent night, holy night,
Son of God, love's pure light
Radiant beams from thy holy face,
With the dawn of redeeming grace,
Jesus, Lord, at thy birth,
Jesus, Lord, at thy birth.

The Animals' Christmas

The Bible story retold by Avril Rowlands
illustrated by Ros Moran

There was a terrible traffic jam at the crossroads in the town of Bethlehem. The ox, tired after his hard day's work in the fields, snorted crossly. When he finally arrived at his stable he was in a bad mood.

'I don't know what's happening, I really don't,' he grumbled, as he came through the door. 'The town's gone mad! Do you know, it took me half an hour to get here from the field? And the noise! Dreadful…' The ox stopped and he stared round the stable. 'Here – what's going on?'

A donkey and two cows stared back at him.

'What are you doing here?' the ox demanded. 'This is *my* stable!'

'Sorry,' said one of the cows. 'There's nowhere else for us to go.'

'What do you mean, nowhere for you to go?' repeated the ox. 'Of course there is. The whole town's full of stables, half empty most of them!'

'My master's been round everywhere. This is the last stable with any room to spare.'

The ox's companion pushed his nose over the edge of his stall. 'What's going on in the town?' he asked quietly.

'Yes,' said one of the cows. 'What *is* going on? Why is Bethlehem so popular all of a sudden? It's not as if it's a holiday resort or a city.'

'I think it's because of the census,' said the donkey.

'What's that?'

'The Romans want to count all the people, so everyone has to go back to the place where they were born.'

'It still doesn't explain what you're all doing in *my* stable,' said the first ox, stubbornly.

'Yes it does,' said the donkey. 'The town's full, so we've been asked to share.'

Just then the stable door burst open.

'Oh close that door, for goodness' sake,' said an owl, calling down from her perch high up in the rafters. 'There's a terrible draught!'

A goat stood just inside the door. 'Sorry,' she bleated.

'I suppose you think you can share my stable tonight,' said the ox.

'Yes please,' said the goat.

'Well you've got another think coming,' said the ox, lowering his head dangerously. 'There's no room.'

'There's plenty of room,' said the goat.

'I don't care if there's all the room in the world!' the ox bellowed. 'This is *my* stable!'

'It's not *your* stable,' said a mouse, running across the floor. 'I live here as well.'

'So do I,' hooted the owl.

'It's my home too,' whispered a spider from the middle of her web.

'What I mean is, I won't have strangers coming in!' said the ox crossly.

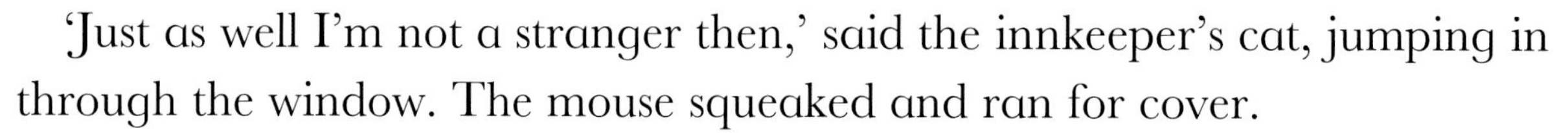

'Just as well I'm not a stranger then,' said the innkeeper's cat, jumping in through the window. The mouse squeaked and ran for cover.

The stable door opened once more and a horse came in.

'Shut that door!' shouted the owl.

The horse looked around the stable. 'Well really,' he complained. 'This is not the kind of accommodation I'm used to.'

'In that case, why don't you go?' said the ox rudely.

'And close the door behind you,' added the owl.

'I'm used to a stall by myself,' said the horse, 'with good fresh hay and a warm blanket to keep out the cold.'

'We're all stuck here for the night,' said the goat, 'so we'd better make the best of it.'

'*I'm* not prepared to make the best of it,' said the ox firmly. 'You seem to forget this is *my* stable!'

'And mine,' said the quiet ox. 'But I don't mind. It's nice to talk to other animals. You can get a bit boring at times.'

'Boring!' gasped the first ox. 'Me? Why you... you...' He lowered his head to charge.

'Now stop that!' said one of the cows in a firm voice. 'I don't like violence. It upsets me and as I'm expecting a baby…'

'That'll make it even more crowded,' giggled the goat.

'If you think this is crowded, you should see the inn!' said the cat. 'At least two to a bed. And the noise! I've come here for a bit of peace and quiet.'

'It doesn't seem like there's going to be much peace in here tonight,' said the donkey, 'and as for quiet…'

'FOR THE LAST TIME, WILL YOU ALL GET OUT!' shouted the ox.

'NO!' the other animals roared back. The cows mooed, the donkey brayed, the goat bleated, the owl hooted, and the mouse brought his excited family in to watch the fun.

'I wish you wouldn't always get so angry,' the quiet ox said to his friend.

But the first ox was not listening. Head down, hooves pawing the ground, he charged. Everyone moved out of the way and the ox would have hit his head against the stable door if it had not suddenly opened. Unable to stop himself, he rushed straight out of the stable, across the courtyard, and landed head first in a large pile of hay.

The animals cheered.

A shabby-looking donkey, patiently waiting to come inside, looked round. 'What was that?' he asked.

'Just my friend,' said the quiet ox. 'Take no notice. I expect you want shelter for the night.'

'Yes please,' said the donkey. 'I do. And my master and mistress too. We've travelled a long way and we're all tired.'

The donkey entered the stable. On his back was a young girl, and a man followed on foot.

The animals looked at the new arrivals.

'Have you come far?' asked the cow.

'From Nazareth,' said the donkey.

The man helped the girl from the donkey's back.

'Oh look,' said the cow, pleased. 'She's expecting a baby, just like me!'

'Ahh,' said the owl. 'I do like babies. I've been quite lonely since mine have grown up and flown the nest.'

The man gathered some straw for a bed and the girl lay down. She smiled up at him, then closed her eyes.

There was a furious pounding on the door.

'That'll be the ox,' sighed the goat. 'I wouldn't let him in if I were you.'

'But it's his stable as well as mine,' said the quiet ox.

The ox burst in, then stopped in amazement. 'What on earth's going on now?'

'I think,' said the owl, 'that the girl is having a baby. Do close the door, and try not to get in the way.'

'Humans?' spluttered the ox. 'In *my* stable?' He shook his head. 'Well, I'm speechless!'

'Thank goodness for that,' said the goat.

It was peaceful in the stable as the baby was born. The only sounds to be heard were the breathing of the animals, the odd shuffling and rustles of straw, and the flutter of wings as the owl flew to and fro.

At last, the baby gave a cry. The animals drew near the rough crib in which he lay. The baby opened his eyes and the animals sank to their knees.

'This,' said the cow, 'is no ordinary baby.'

Everyone was silent, even the ox. But soon the peace was broken by a loud banging. The door burst open and in walked three shepherds, followed by their sheep.

'Well really!' exclaimed the ox. 'They barge in without a "by your leave" or a "would you mind?" Some people have no manners!'

But he no longer sounded cross. Neither did the owl, who ruffled her feathers as she said, 'Close that door, we don't want the baby to catch cold!'

A Golden Gift Box

A Christmas poem illustrated by Elena Gomez

It's Christmas time,
When angels come
To earth from heaven above.
Take a golden gift box
And fill it full of love.

It's Christmas time!
The angels' song
Is heard upon the ground.
Open up the gift box,
Let love shine all around.

The Good Samaritan

A retelling of Jesus' parable illustrated by Gail Newey

One day, a teacher of God's law came up to Jesus. He wanted to trap him with a clever question that Jesus wouldn't be able to answer. 'Teacher,' he asked, 'what must I do to receive eternal life?'

Jesus asked him, 'What do the scriptures say? How do you explain what you read in them?'

The man quoted the ancient writings of the Jewish people: ' "Love the Lord your God with all your heart, with all your soul, with all your strength, and with all your mind" and "Love your neighbour as you love yourself." '

'You are right,' said Jesus. 'Do this, and you will live.'

But the man was annoyed that Jesus had dealt with his question so cleverly and so quickly. So he asked another question: 'Who is my neighbour?'

Jesus answered with a story:

'There was once a man who was travelling down the road from Jerusalem to Jericho. There, in a lonely spot, robbers attacked him, stripped him and beat him up, leaving him half-dead.

'It so happened that a priest, who led the worship of God in the Temple in Jerusalem, was going down that road. When he saw the man, he walked by on the other side of the road.

'Then a Levite came, an assistant in the very same Temple. He went up to the man and looked at him. Then he, too, walked by on the other side.

'Finally a Samaritan came along.'

Jesus paused for a moment. His listeners were left wondering, 'Why has he chosen to bring a Samaritan into his story? Our people despise the Samaritans! They do not respect our Temple in Jerusalem as they should – and that is clear evidence that they don't worship God in the right way!'

Jesus continued the story: 'When the Samaritan saw the injured man, he was filled with pity for him. He went over to him, poured oil and wine on his wounds and bandaged them. Then he lifted the man onto his donkey and took him to an inn, where he took care of him.

'The next day he took out two silver coins and gave them to the innkeeper. "Take care of him," he told the innkeeper. "When I return this way, I will pay you whatever else you spend on him." '

Then Jesus asked, 'In your opinion, which one of these three acted like a neighbour towards the man attacked by the robbers?'

The teacher of the Law answered, 'The one who was kind to him.'

Jesus replied, 'You go, then, and do likewise.'

Simple Prayers

Three prayers from the Amish tradition
illustrated by Katarzyna Klein

I am only me, but I'm still someone.
I cannot do everything, but I can do something.
Just because I cannot do everything does not
give me the right to do nothing.

O God,

We give thanks for the goodhearted people
who love us and do good to us and who
show their mercy and kindness by providing
us with food and drink, house and shelter
when we are in trouble or in need.

O God,

May there be nothing in this day's work
of which we shall be ashamed when the sun has
set, nor in the eventide of our life when our task
is done and we go to our long home to meet
you face to face.
Amen.

The Lost Sheep

Jesus' parable retold by Meryl Doney
illustrated by Graham Round

One day Jesus' friends asked him: 'Who does God love most?'

'My father loves everyone,' said Jesus. He pointed to a little child. 'Children are not big and strong. They trust their parents to look after them. My father wants people to trust him and love him just like that. He will look after them.'

'What if they go away from God, and don't love him?' asked one of Jesus' friends.

So Jesus told this story...

Once upon a time, there was a shepherd who had a hundred sheep. He looked after them. He found them grass to eat and water to drink.

At night he led them safely home to their sheep pen. The shepherd counted them as they went in through the gate.

One night he counted and there were only ninety-nine sheep. One sheep was lost. The shepherd was very worried. He set off at once to look for the sheep. He took with him his shepherd's stick and a bag of food. He called to the sheep as he walked.

Soon it was dark. But still the shepherd searched among the rocks and prickly bushes.

Suddenly, the shepherd heard a feeble bleat. It was his sheep crying.

He ran towards the sound. There was his sheep, caught in the bushes! He used his shepherd's stick to get her out. Then he took her in his arms. He carried her back to the sheep pen on his shoulders. The ninety-nine sheep were safe inside, waiting for him.

Gently the shepherd put his lost sheep down with the others. She was so glad to be back home. She skipped and jumped for joy. The shepherd was glad, too. He hurried to tell all his friends.

'I have found my lost sheep. I am going to have a party,' he said. Some brought pipes and drums to make music. Others sang and danced. It was a wonderful party. Everyone was glad the sheep had been found.

... and she was glad to be safe home again, too.

'My father is like that shepherd,' said Jesus. 'He knows us all by name. If one of us goes away from him, he will come to look for us, because he loves us. When he brings us back, he is as glad as the shepherd in my story.'

The Lord's Prayer

Jesus' prayer presented and retold by Lois Rock
illustrated by Debbie Lush

The Lord's prayer was taught by Jesus to his followers.

He said that the God of the universe longs to welcome everyone with love and laughter and he told his followers how they could speak to God in prayer, as a child speaks to a parent whom they can love and trust.

Our Father, who art in heaven,

Are we alone in a vast, spinning universe…
or does someone watch over us, as a parent watches
over a child?

hallowed be thy Name.

And if there is a someone, then that Someone must
be strong, life-giving, gentle, good and loving.

Thy kingdom come,

So may goodness and love rule in this world.

Thy will be done, on Earth as it is in Heaven.

May goodness and love rule through all the universe, both seen and unseen.

Give us this day our daily bread.

May the world's people have all they need to live in simplicity and joy.

And forgive us our trespasses,

When we fail to be good and loving, may we be forgiven.

as we forgive those who trespass against us.

When we are wronged, may we learn to forgive.

And lead us not into temptation,

May we never fall prey to hatred, greed and wickedness.

but deliver us from evil:

May we be safe from anything that might dishearten or destroy us.

For thine is the kingdom, the power and the glory,
for ever and ever. Amen.

Picnic in the Hills

The story of the feeding of the five thousand
retold by Timothy Dudley-Smith
illustrated by Terry Gabbey

To this day, nobody knows his name. He was just a boy who lived over the hills by the Sea of Galilee. One fine afternoon his mother sent him out with a picnic supper in his pocket, and told him to be sure and come home before dark.

On the hillside by the lake, to his great surprise, he found a crowd of people – more people than he had ever seen in his life before. There were farmers and peasants, women and children, babies and dogs, all sitting on the green grass in the late spring sunshine, listening to Jesus. As Jesus looked at them, he loved them and his heart went out to them. They were his fellow-countrymen. He told them how God loved them too.

By the time he had finished speaking, the sun was low in the sky, and it was growing cold. The twelve disciples urged Jesus to send the people home. It was late, they said, and most of them were tired and hungry, and some had a long way to go. But because he loved them, Jesus said they must first have supper; then they should go home.

The puzzled disciples did not know what to do when they heard this. They had no food with them, and there was nowhere nearby where they could buy any. Only the boy from over the hills had his picnic supper – and he shyly offered that to Andrew if it was any help. And so as not to disappoint him, Andrew told Jesus. There were five thousand hungry people waiting; and here were five little barley rolls and two small dried fish. Jesus looked at them, and looked at Andrew, and looked at the boy; and then he told the disciples to make the crowd sit down again.

By now they had all begun to get up and stretch their legs and collect their children and start for home; but before long the disciples had them all sitting down again, in neat rows on the green hillside.

Jesus took the napkin with the five rolls and the two dried fish, and looked up to heaven and said a prayer, thanking God for the food. And then he began to break the food up with his fingers, and give it in handfuls to the twelve disciples, for them to carry it to the crowd. Handful after handful after handful – and still there was more.

In the end, there was enough for everyone – and a lot left over if anyone had wanted more. Happy and fed and satisfied, the people drifted home. The boy, too, full of fish and barley bread, walked slowly home in the twilight, his mind busy with what he had heard and seen. Perhaps, too, he was thinking to himself that if you give even a very little into the hands of Jesus, there is no knowing what he can do with it.

Make Me a Channel of Your Peace

The Saint Francis prayer illustrated by Alison Wisenfeld

Lord, make me a channel of your peace.
Where there is hatred, let me sow love,
Where there is injury, pardon,
Where there is doubt, faith,
Where there is despair, hope,
Where there is darkness, light,
Where there is sadness, joy.

O Divine Master, grant that I may not
so much seek to be consoled as to console,
not so much to be understood as to understand,
not so much to be loved as to love;
for it is in giving that we receive,
it is in pardoning that we are pardoned,
it is in dying that we awake to eternal life.

Jesus and the Man Who Was Rescued

A retelling of the story of Jesus and Zaccheus
illustrated by Roger Langton

Long ago, in a town called Jericho, lived a man named Zaccheus.

He was very, very rich.

But no one liked him. No one wanted to talk to him. No one wanted to go to his house.

Poor Zaccheus! Why didn't he have any friends?

Was it something to do with his job? Zaccheus was a tax collector. He collected money from people and gave it to the Romans who ruled the land.

And the Romans told him to collect a little extra for his own wages.

Everyone knew that Zaccheus collected a lot more than he needed to give the Romans.

He kept lots and lots of money for himself.

One day, Jesus came to Jericho. Jesus! The man who could make sick people well; the man everyone wanted to hear.

Lots of people wanted to see him.

Zaccheus wanted to see Jesus too. But he was short.

There were so many people in front of him, that he could not see anything.

So he did a clever thing. He ran ahead, and climbed a tree. Now he could see what was going on.

And Jesus was coming that way.

Jesus came to the tree, and stopped. He looked up and said, 'Hurry down, Zaccheus. I must stay in your house today.'

Zaccheus came down very fast. He was so happy! Someone wanted to visit him at last.

Lots of the other people there were angry.

'It's not fair,' they grumbled. 'Jesus is going to the house of a cheat – the man who makes himself rich and leaves us poor.'

Zaccheus and Jesus had a meal together. And they talked.

Something in what Jesus said and did made Zaccheus want to change his ways.

He stood up and said to Jesus, 'Listen. I will give half of all I have to the poor.

'If I have cheated anyone, I will pay them back four times as much.'

Jesus was happy. 'My work is to rescue people who have lost their way in life,' he said. 'And today, someone in this house has been rescued.'

God Cares for Me

Two prayers illustrated by John Wallace

God, who made the earth,
The air, the sky, the sea,
Who gave the light its birth,
Careth for me.

God, who made the grass,
The flower, the fruit, the tree,
The day and night to pass,
Careth for me.

God, who made all things,
On earth, in air, in sea,
Who changing seasons brings,
Careth for me.

Sarah Betts Rhodes

When I am in a temper
When I get really mad
I can be very dangerous
I can be very bad.

I'm wild as a tiger
I'm wild as a bear
I'm wilder than a wildebeest
And I don't even care.

Dear God who made the tiger
Dear God who made the bear
Please let me know you love me still
And that you'll always care.

Mark Robinson

Sad News, Glad News

A retelling of the Easter story
illustrated by Louise Rawlings

Long, long ago and far away
Was born a baby boy:
The baby Jesus. Angels said
He came to bring us joy.

Jesus grew to be a man.
He was both good and kind:
He healed those who were ill and sad
And gave sight to the blind.

He told of God, who made the world
And loves both great and small;
Who clothes the flowers, who feeds the birds,
Who takes care of us all.

He said that God is overjoyed
When people turn from wrong.
And when they live as God's friends should,
The angels join in song.

But some grew angry at these words:
'That man,' they said, 'must die.'
They whispered, plotted, lied – and had him
Nailed to a cross so high.

The sky grew dark: it might have seemed
That only bad would live.
But Jesus looked upon the world
And said to God, 'Forgive.'

Then Jesus' friends, all weeping,
Laid his body in a tomb.
They rolled the stone door closed
And spent the next day deep in gloom.

Another day: the friends returned
To say a last goodbye.
But who had rolled the stone door back
Before dawn lit the sky?

And then they saw them:
angels bright,
Who said, 'You must not cry.
For Jesus is alive again –
God's love can never die.'

So celebrate glad Easter news:
All bad things are forgiven.
God's gentle love fills all the world
And Jesus Christ is risen.

The Land that Breaks Beyond Our Dreams

A poem by Stewart Henderson
illustrated by Christopher Corr

The land that breaks
beyond our dreams
has crocuses that do not dip
below the earth of winter;
and it is only their mood there
which makes the petals cup in prayer
or spread with joy.

The land that breaks
beyond our dreams
only breathes the virgin air
of itself, and the roaming rainbows
of its ribbon afternoons;
when the birdsong scoops the
too-long dead from our
mean, untidy graves.

The land that breaks
beyond our dreams
is where the drained begin to leap
and the faint rustle of the
butterfly's waltz
is enough to kneel you deep,
tame with yourself
and sluiced of all your woes.

The land that breaks
beyond our dreams
where all that glory comes beside us,
and surging shoals of daffodils
surf across an ocean, or,
perhaps a cloud;
that will be when
there is no more proud;
and the missing, the mad,
and the cowed,
will know how to sing descant
with the voice behind the nightingale.

The Easter Story

A retelling from the Bible illustrated by Jackie Morris

For three years Jesus went about his work of helping and healing, and many people loved him.

The scribes and the Pharisees hated him. They wanted to have him put to death, but they were afraid to do so, because he had so great a following. Perhaps they could have him put to death secretly?

Then came the chance they had been waiting for: at the time of a great festival known as Passover, Jesus and his followers came to the city of Jerusalem. One of Jesus' close friends told them where they could come and arrest him. One night, as he prayed to God in an olive grove named Gethsemane, soldiers came and hustled Jesus away.

They told lies about him. They made up a story that he planned to rebel against the Romans who ruled the land. The Roman governor did not really believe the story, but Jesus'

enemies had done their work well. When the governor offered to set Jesus free, the crowd had turned against him. 'Crucify him, crucify him,' they shouted.

Roman soldiers took their orders. They whipped Jesus. They stripped him of his clothes. They led him to a hillside outside the city and laid him on a cross

of wood. Then they drove great iron nails through his hands and feet and stood the cross upright in the ground.

On the day that Jesus was crucified, two other men – both criminals – were led out to die. They were crucified, one on Jesus' right, one on Jesus' left.

Jesus said a prayer to God.

'Father, forgive them, they don't know what they are doing.'

The leaders of the people jeered at Jesus. 'He saved others. Let's see if he can save himself.'

The soldiers mocked him. 'You are charged with wanting to be the king of your own people. Save yourself if you're so great!'

One of the criminals hurled insults at him. 'Aren't you meant to be the one sent by God to save our people? If you are, then save yourself and us.'

But the other man spoke sharply. 'Beware of God,' he warned. 'We are getting the due punishment for our crime. This man is getting the same punishment, yet he has done no wrong.'

He spoke to Jesus: 'Remember me when you come as King.'

And Jesus replied, 'I promise you that today you will be in paradise with me.'

It was about twelve o'clock on the day Jesus was crucified that the sun stopped shining. Darkness covered the whole country until three o'clock.

Jesus called out to God in a loud voice, 'Father! Into your hands I place my spirit!' He said this and died.

Now, among the powerful religious people who had plotted against Jesus were some who had not agreed with what had been done. One of these was a rich man named Joseph, who came from the town of Arimathea.

He asked for permission to take the body of Jesus. He took it down from the cross, wrapped it in a linen sheet and placed it in a tomb cut like a cave out of solid rock. A round stone door was rolled in place over the entrance.

There was no time to prepare the body properly for its burial, for now the sun was setting and the sabbath day of rest was beginning.

Joseph and the others who had come to the tomb with him went away, in deepest sorrow. It seemed that they would never sing and dance again.

Very early on Sunday morning, the women who had gathered to watch as Jesus was laid in the tomb returned.

They brought the spices that were used in preparing a body for burial.

They found the stone rolled away from the entrance to the tomb. Stooping a little, they went inside.

To their astonishment, the tomb was empty. The body simply was not there.

Suddenly two people in bright shining clothes stood by them. The women bowed down to the ground in fear, but then the people spoke: 'Why are you looking among the dead for one who is alive? He is not here; he has been raised to life. Remember what he said: he told you he would be crucified and then would rise again.'

The women remembered Jesus' words. But that was not all. As the day went by, people saw him with their own eyes.

For many days afterwards, Jesus appeared among groups of his astonished followers. He talked with them. He ate with them. He showed them the marks of the nails in his body… he was truly Jesus, yet somehow different – more alive than ever before.

After forty days, Jesus said goodbye. He told his friends not to worry: even though they would no longer see him, he would come close to them in a new and special way.

Then Jesus was taken up to heaven. As his closest followers watched, a cloud hid him from their sight.

Bedtime Blessings

Five prayers illustrated by Kath Lucas

Jesus, friend
of little children,
Be a friend to me;
Take my hand
and ever keep me
Close to thee.

Walter J. Mathams

God bless all those
that I love;
God bless all those
that love me;
God bless all those
that love those that I love,
And all those
that love those that love me.

New England sampler

Now I lay me
down to sleep,
I pray thee, Lord,
thy child to keep;
Thy love to guard me
through the night
And wake me in
the morning light.

Traditional

Dear Father, hear and bless
Thy beasts and singing birds
And guard with tenderness
Small things that have no words.

Sleep, my child,
and peace attend thee,
All through the night;
Guardian angels
God will send thee,
All through the night;
Soft the drowsy
hours are creeping,
Hill and vale
in slumber sleeping,
I my loving vigil keeping,
All through the night.

Traditional Welsh prayer

Published by
Lion Publishing plc
Sandy Lane West, Oxford, England
www.lion-publishing.co.uk
ISBN 0 7459 4711 5

First edition 2001
10 9 8 7 6 5 4 3 2 1

A catalogue record for this book is available
from the British Library

Typeset in Baskerville MT Schoolbook
Printed and bound in Singapore

Acknowledgments
Cover (clockwise from top left): Katarzyna Klein, Christopher Corr, Francesca Pelizzoli, Debbie Lush, Alex Ayliffe, Jill Newton, Ros Moran, Liz Pichon, John Wallace, Gail Newey. Copyright © individual illustrators listed above.
In the Beginning: first published as a picture story book with this title in 1997. Text copyright © 1996 Steve Turner. Illustrations copyright © 1997 Jill Newton.
Thank You for Our World: prayers selected from *Prayers for a Fragile World*, written and compiled by Carol Watson and first published in 1991, copyright © 1991 Lion Publishing. 'Father, thank you for the sun' by Alexander Carter, 'Thank you, Lord, for our world' by Naomi Smith. Illustrations copyright © 1991 Rhian Nest James.
My Very First Noah's Ark Story: first published as a board book with this title in 2001. Text copyright © 2001 Lion Publishing. Illustrations copyright © 2001 Alex Ayliffe.
A Prayer of Thanksgiving: selected from *A Child's Book of Celtic Prayers*, written and compiled by Joyce Denham and first published in 1998. Text copyright © 1998 Joyce Denham. Illustrations copyright © 1998 Helen Cann.
Mabel and the Tower of Babel: first published as a picture story book with this title in 1990. Text and illustrations copyright © 1990 John Ryan.
Joseph: first published as part of *My Little Box of Bible Friends* in 1991. Text copyright © 1991 Lion Publishing. Illustrations copyright © 1991 Toni Goffe.
Moses Hears God's Call: a story selected from *The Lion Children's Bible*, first published in 1981 with illustrations by Carolyn Cox from the second edition published in 1991. Text copyright © 1981 and 1991 Pat Alexander (text adapted for this anthology). Illustrations copyright © 1991 Carolyn Cox.
The Ten Commandments: first published as a prayer book called *The Ten Commandments for Children* in 1995. Copyright © 1995 Lion Publishing. Illustrations copyright © 1995 Claire Henley.
The Knock-out Story of David and Goliath: first published as a picture story book with this title in 2000. Copyright © 2000 Lion Publishing. Illustrations copyright © 2000 Bernice Lum.
A Happy Day: prayers selected from *Prayers for Special Days*, *Everyday Prayers* and *Goodnight Prayers*, first published in 1993. Illustrations copyright © 1993 Maureen Bradley.
A Fishy Story: selected from *The Lion First Bible*, first published in 1997. Text copyright © 1997 Pat Alexander. Illustrations copyright © 1997 Leon Baxter.
My Boat and Me: a prayer selected from *Twilight Verses, Moonlight Rhymes* compiled by Mary Joslin and first published in 1997. Copyright © 1997 Lion Publishing. Illustrations copyright © 1997 Liz Pichon.
Daniel and the Lions: a story selected from *The Lion Storyteller Bible*, first published in 1995. Text copyright © 1995 Bob Hartman. Illustrations copyright © 1995 Susie Poole.
The World is Such a Wonderful Place: prayers selected from *The Lion Treasury of Children's Prayers*, compiled by Susan Cuthbert and first published in 1999. Text by Mary Batchelor. Illustrations copyright © 1999 Alison Jay.
The First Christmas: first published as one of the *Lion Story Bible* series in 1986. Copyright © 1986 Lion Publishing. Illustrations copyright © 1986 John Haysom.
Silent Night: first published in this arrangement in *Best-Loved Carols* in 1998 and with Francesca Pelizzoli's illustrations in *Celebrating Christmas* in 1998. Arrangement of Franz Grüber's 'Silent Night' copyright © 1998 Philip and Victoria Tebbs. Illustrations copyright © 1998 Francesca Pelizzoli.
The Animal's Christmas: adapted from *The Animals' Christmas and Other Stories*, first published in 1997 and in this retelling with Rosslyn Moran's illustrations in *The Christmas Sheep and Other Stories*, published in 2000. Text copyright © 2000 Avril Rowlands. Illustrations copyright © 2000 Rosslyn Moran.
A Golden Gift Box: a poem selected from *Celebrating Christmas*, first published in 1998. Copyright © 1998 Lion Publishing. Illustrations copyright © 1998 Elena Gomez.
The Good Samaritan: selected from *Best-Loved Parables*, first published in 1998. Copyright © 1998 Lion Publishing. Illustrations copyright © 1998 Gail Newey.
Simple Prayers: selected from a prayer book with this title compiled by Lois Rock, first published in 2001. Illustrations copyright © 2001 Katarzyna Klein.
The Lost Sheep: first published as a picture story book with this title in 1979. Text copyright © 1979 and 1980 Lion Publishing. Illustrations copyright © 1979 and 1980 Graham Round.
The Lord's Prayer: first published as a prayer book with this title in 1999. Copyright © 1999 Lion Publishing. Illustrations copyright © 1999 Debbie Lush.
Picnic in the Hills: selected from *The Lion Book of Stories of Jesus*, first published in 1971 and with Terry Gabbey's illustrations in 1986. Text copyright © 1971, 1986 Timothy Dudley-Smith. Illustrated edition copyright © 1986 Lion Publishing.
Make Me a Channel of Your Peace: selected from *The Good Man of Assisi*, written by Mary Joslin and first published in 1997. Illustrations copyright © 1997 Alison Wisenfeld.
Jesus and the Man Who Was Rescued: first published as a picture story book with this title in 1997 and as part of *A Little Life of Jesus* in 1997. Copyright © 1996, 1997 Lion Publishing. Illustrations copyright © 1996 Roger Langton.
God Cares for Me: prayers selected from *Prayers to Know By Heart*, first published in 2000. 'When I am in a temper' copyright © 2000 Lion Publishing. Illustrations copyright © 2000 John Wallace.
Sad News, Glad News: first published as a prayer book with this title in 1997. Copyright © 1997 Lion Publishing. Illustrations copyright © 1997 Louise Rawlings.
The Land that Breaks Beyond Our Dreams: poem reproduced from the collection *Limited Edition* (Plover Books, 1997) and first published by Lion in *Heaven in a Poem*, compiled by Lois Rock in 2000. Text copyright © 1997 Stewart Henderson. Illustrations copyright © 2000 Christopher Corr.
The Easter Story: extracted from a story book entitled *Lord of the Dance*, first published in 1998. Story text copyright © 1998 Lion Publishing. Illustrations copyright © 1998 Jackie Morris.
Bedtime Blessings: 'Jesus, friend of little children', 'God bless all those that I love', 'Now I lay me down to sleep', 'Dear Father, hear and bless' selected from *Bedtime Blessings* compiled by Sophie Piper and first published in 2000. 'Sleep, my child, and peace attend thee' from *Heavenly Angels* compiled by Sophie Piper and first published in 2000. Illustrations copyright © 2000 Kath Lucas.

All Lion books are available from your local bookshop, or can be ordered via our website or from Marston Book Services. For a free catalogue, showing the complete list of titles available, please contact:

Customer Services
Marston Book Services Ltd
PO Box 269
160 Milton Park Estate
Abingdon
Oxon
OX14 4YN

Tel: 01235 465500
Fax: 01235 465555

Our website can be found at:
www.lion-publishing.co.uk